Rebel Soldiers

and other musings on the vanity of life.

By
Terry R. Freeman

Cover Photo by Author: Spotsylvania Confederate
Cemetery, Spotsylvania, Virginia - May 16, 2006

ISBN: 978-0-6151-8020-5

Tóg bog é Publishing
Snellville, Georgia

Dedication

This book is dedicated to three people: my wife Judy, my son Nate, and my daughter-in-law Melody.

My precious wife Judy has always believed in me when I didn't believe in myself.

My son Nate he has always encouraged me. He continues to be a constant source of joy and pride in my life.

Last but by no means least my "Baby Girl" Melody is a beautiful, wonderful daughter to me. Her strength of purpose and gentle spirit inspire me.

I love you all. My life is richer because of you.

Terry R. Freeman
November 2007

Contents

I'm Getting Older

I think about death now.
I didn't used to.
I believed death would never make me bow.
Didn't older people have anything better to do
than to read the obituaries in the newspaper?

My death thoughts are not of a morbid sense.
But I admit that they do cross my mind.
I'm not that dense,
but as I get older I feel a little behind
if I don't check out the "obits" myself.

You never know.
I see people my age in there all the time.
I know I'm ready if it's my time to go,
but if it's all the same to you I'll go on a later
climb.
Jacob's Ladder is usually a one-way trip.

Simplicity

The longer I live the more I am convinced that simplicity is the key to happiness.

In this techno-complex world in which we live it is hard to accept that less is best.

Stress moves in on every side and we really have to work to find a moment's peace it seems.

I wonder what would happen if we left our computers and their kind and went off to chase our dreams.

Go out and buy a Harley and blast off in search of America, or some other unknown shore.

Take off your helmet if you dare and feel the wind flowing through what little hair you have; it's just beyond the door.

Or maybe your dream is to fly away and leave this world and go trekking among the stars.

Or Marrakech. Yeah that's it. With its narrow Moroccan streets and mysterious, smoke-filled bars.

Technology's spell makes us unable to get out of our own way.

Slowly our brain cells have started to decay.

Do things that break technology's sway: Read a book, write a letter, take a trip in your imagination; do it today.

Spring

I took a walk in the warmth of the sun,

and as I looked around I saw work to be done.

I sensed that Old Man Winter had let us slip from his hold.

He was back in the Arctic where it's always snowy and cold.

There were shrubs to be trimmed and flower beds to weed.

The patchy front lawn was in need of some seed.

Tree limbs lay willy-nilly around all about.

Yes, there was work to be done I had no doubt.

So I rolled up my sleeves and attacked all the tasks.

One by one they where finished till I came to the last,

and I finished it too, not being one to quit.

Then I looked all around. Good work; I was so proud of it.

I took a walk in the warmth of the sun,

and when I looked around there was no work to be done.

Reconnection

Riding through the heartland along Georgia's eastern back roads.

The corn is so green it looks black and the dirt is gray.

The black and white Holsteins look as though they've been scattered across the bright green hillocks by the hand of God.

The silos point like stubby fingers toward the sky on the Mennonite farms.

Their simple churches and simpler faith knit the fabric of land and flesh together.

I notice a doe standing in the edge of a cotton field.

Timidly waiting for me to pass.

The bright, reddish color of her coat against the dark brown-green pine forest is beautiful.

Off in the distance an anvil-head rises toward Heaven preparing to bless the hot afternoon with its gift.

It is a pastoral scene; Peace defined in nature's majesty.

I sigh a contented sigh.

I feel connected to my roots and myself again.

That which was thought to be lost was rediscovered in the beauty of an early summer, Georgia afternoon.

Birmingham (Inspired by Bruce Cockburn)

Shadows are steamy pools around feet at midday
that slowly elongate toward the oncoming night.
The heat is oppressive in Birmingham in
summer.
The streetlamps flicker, grudgingly giving up
light.

Orange bright circles perfect on the cooling
pavement.
That hot, sticky asphalt smell is still there though
fading.
The black and white cruiser creeps up as if
wanting to
take a look at the sight standing between
them…waiting.

The window is down and the officer chuckles as
he
drives on not certain what he's seen, but
bemused.
The laughter is slowly fading like the glow in the
West.
Keep moving, because there isn't anything left to
lose.

Behind the mountain in Birmingham and in
August

the wind's breath is like the open door of a
furnace

in one of the few rusting old steel mills out on
the edge of town.

Vulcan is silent…His stern demeanor offers no
solace.

Moving or standing still it's all the same in
Birmingham

in Summer when the loud rain refuses to offer its
relief.

Away from town the cool darkness is total and
complete.

Shuffling on the Thunderbird wrestles with the
grief.

Old Friends

We move in different circles now

Elliptical and ever further apart

and yet when our courses do intersect

we discover we are still connected at the heart.

Past experiences shared galvanize us

Sealing and protecting our friendship from life's
storms.

Sight is not necessary for communion

when constant presence in thought is the norm.

The incidents and accidents of living move us
further on

toward the opening of that final door.

Passage will cause one of us pain,

but the other will know that none has loved him
more.

The Old Road

The old road meandered along at the side of the
new

as if it were lost and searching for its way.

Serpentine; first on the left side and then on the
right

as far as I could see into the approaching night.

It was overcome by briars, brambles and creeping
vine.

Following me in silence, but if it were able to
speak

many fascinating stories I am sure it would love
to tell.

The moist fall air hung low and heavy with a
woodsy smell.

My imagination painted many vivid pictures on
the old road;

of marching red-coated soldiers and their
protected immigrants.

Cautiously making their way inland from the
lonely rugged coast

as falling leaves of varying hues fluttered to the
ground to rest.

Then Sherman's mighty army lumbered past in
the opposite direction

toward Savannah on their terrible March to the
Sea.

The stolen mules and other livestock nosily
followed along;

"The Battle Hymn of the Republic" was their
marshaling song.

As darkness fell softly over the gently rolling hills

it jolted me back to the reality of the present day.

The old road was no longer visible in the
increasing twilight.

I left its memories behind as I drove into the
coming night.

Point Loma

The sun dipped his feet into the sea as if to
check its temperature before venturing in.
Satisfied, he slipped his bottom slowly,
ever so slowly beneath the cool sea water.
The swirling clouds on the horizon looked
like steam hovering over his evening swim.
Colors changed subtly and he sank deeper.
Bright yellow became a translucent orange
and pinkish reds appeared around the edges
of the steam, or was it clouds? I'm not sure.
The old lighthouse watched the scene from
the heights of the cliff overlooking the harbor.
What moments ago appeared so detailed now
looks like a shadow drawing; two dimensional.
The pale orange glow on the horizon signals
the end of another beautiful day at Point Loma
as the sun slips quietly beneath the waves.

Autumn

The multi-colored leaves fall

tumbling and floating as they do.

Chilly winds blow, skipping them along the
ground.

Autumn has arrived.

Little children run and jump into piles of leaves,

scattering those their father has raked with glee.

The clear blue sky is streaked with smoke as the
leaves are burned.

The smell of Autumn fills the air.

Autumn always brings back memories of another
place.

Another time.

The foolish actions of a young man so very long
ago,

but nothing can be changed.

Autumn has arrived.

Tell "Hoppy" I'll Be There Soon

One by one their voices have fallen silent, victims of the passage of time.

Yet their faces still hover in my memory like fog over a swamp at dawn.

I miss you companions of my youth like I miss my comfortable clothes

that are taken in the night by thieves; at least they've disappeared.

Your images remain flickering in a medium of half tone gray and black.

Pictures that take me back to a simpler time of sweet childhood joy.

Granny waiting at the door when I got off of the school bus with her

tea cakes and a glass of cold, cold milk; I can't believe she's be gone too.

I rode with you before homework on reruns, and after it in prime time.

Before the days of color television and rock and roll brought the changes.

Recess at school was filled with talk of you, and many hours were spent

pretending I was you in the grassless front yard; only lazy folks had grass.

I've grown older and I haven't seen you in a while: I've spent as much time

as I could with you, or at least as much time as adulthood would allow.

I am standing at the top of the hill now and you just went around the curve.

I can still hear the hoof beats of your horse; tell "Hoppy" I'll be there soon.

The Dark Side

There is a dark side to everyone.
A place where life is inane and meaningless.
It is a cold and bitter habitation
that has never felt the warmth of the sun.

Some of us go there frequently.
Others have no recollection of its existence,
but it is there just the same;
even if we don't want it to be.

The secret is to not to set up housekeeping
in its dank and foreboding confines.
Citizenship in the dark side is costly.
Paid for with the very essence of your being.

A View of Life From the Pacific Coast Highway

I was moved today deep within my mind and spirit.

Looking out at the peaceful emerald-green Pacific

an ancient, until then unknown, long dead idea's fire was lit.

The waves had somehow kindled the neglected wick.

High upon the hill I stood alone stark still

locked and lost in the sea's unending motion.

My spirit man watched with passive interest as the windmill

of my mind which turned, fascinated with the notion.

The sea was calm farther out and a lone ship's sails were bright.

I laughed out loud at all of her efforts to tack.

If man is a ship on life's sea, sailing in search of light

then love is the wind we struggle to keep at our back.

Human emotions make up the sail's fragile fabric

and our faith is the mast against which it strains.

Charting a safe course through life's rocks is the trick

for our sea is filled with dreams, and also many pains.

A True Christian (For my friend, Bill Meng)

True Christianity is more than stained glass
windows and dark wood.

It is a deeply centered principle that drives
everything we strive to be.

I've known many "Christians" who didn't really
know where they stood;

So deep in bondage to laws and others'
expectations unable to break free.

Pomp and circumstance are just that and nothing
more,

and talk is cheap and meaningless if the life you
live isn't true.

To learn to walk in peace and let our spirits on
the wings of eagles soar

is the essence of God's truth and the rudder
should guide everything we do.

Once in a while in this life if you are blessed you
find someone true to the end.

A person who quietly lives their Christianity for
all of the world to see.

I knew a man like that and I'm honored to have called him a friend.

His quiet witness remain an inspiration to me.

I watched him live his faith in the greatest of life's trials

when his integrity, honor and ability were questioned by many.

Through all of the heartache and pain he was silent and managed to smile,

And though I know he wrestled with the enemy Bitterness I never saw any.

He focused on the important things of life like his family and his God,

and when the storm was raging he stood calmly smiling at seeming disaster.

His detractors couldn't understand this and thought him very odd,

but he uttered not a word and refused to let their attacks become his master.

If true success is found in the life lived measured against words spoken,

a winner defined by the number of people he touches, not races won,

then he was both and his faith sustained him till
he left us all too soon, unbroken;

Bill Meng, a true Christian known by his love
given away and the things he's done.

Summer Thoughts

I used to walk along red dirt country roads.

I loved those sweet breezes of honeysuckle wind.

The hot sun blistered the tops of my feet.

The dust I kicked up drifted off through the tall pines.

Summertime in Georgia.

Happy times of my youth.

Lazy days on the banks of the Yellow River; Zebco in hand.

The feel of the worms as they squirm in my fingers;

in their futile attempts to avoid my Eagle Claw.

Catfish and bluegill bites.

Long, satisfying drinks of the cool river water.

I go back there in my mind. Often.

By my summer thoughts I am convinced that flowing streams and lazy dreams are all that is real.

It is life that is an illusion.

I Wait

I wait.

In waiting I eventually find peace.

Peace that brings release.

I struggle as I wait, but

I wait.

I wait.

Though often I don't seem to see.

Seeing won't set me free.

I must struggle deep inside so

I wait.

I wait.

My strength is waning, almost gone

yet I must continue on.

I struggle and I rest and

I wait.

I wait. I wait. I wait.

The Old Man's Death

The earth, at a leisurely pace, is warmed by the
sun

yet seemingly overnight its beauty comes into
focus.

Flowers are timidly peeking up through the
lingering

blanket of snow, and hyacinths appear with the
crocus.

Bird songs fill the air outside my window and I
am

compelled to fling it open wide and let them in.

The mocking bird's call is the first I hear but
soon he

is joined by many, too many to identify in the
din.

I venture outside into the melting snow to take in
the

evolving scene that unfolds before my winter-
hungry eyes.

Winter gives way grudgingly to his young friend
Spring

and quietly, almost without a sound, the old man
dies.

No time for mourning him because I am glad
he's gone.

I shall not miss his cold, icy breath that chills me
so.

No I shall not miss him in the least and what's
more,

the truth be told, I am very glad to finally see him
go.

Questions

In the early dawn a beautiful sunrise peeks over the horizon like a timid child.

As I watch the colors explode in the distance to bring about another new day.

What will it hold?

Questions of life that need to be answered but are left without any.

The poison of selfishness has crept into my mind and tried to destroy friendships that once were dear.

Where will it end?

Time and time alone will solve the problems and calm the tempers that flared.

Things that aren't should be, and things that are should never have been.

Why?

A Typical Winter's Day

The sky was the color of pewter and a cold rain fell like the

spray that flies when the ocean crashes upon the rocks.

The trees poked their steely fingers at the clouds as if

imploring them to hold their moisture until a more convenient time.

Oak leaves danced on the wind swirling higher and higher

then floated back down to land softly on the cold wet ground.

The garden spot, so green and inviting in summer, lay dormant;

Its remains brown and cloddy amid the tan colored grass.

The blueberry bushes were almost bear except for a few

tenacious berries that held fast in defiance of winter's chill.

The lone red cedar stood verdant against a background of

whites and browns of the sleeping trees all around it.

The blue birds flirted with their house constantly rearranging its

contents in preparation and in anticipation of the coming spring.

I watched them for a while as the light began to fade then turned

and headed back inside to the warm fire of a typical winter's day.

There Are Only Plastic Flowers Where I Am Going

The beauty of this world has made me sad
because I shall not partake of it for long.
You see life is a fleeting vapor that at its
thickest disappears and is gone without a trace.

When my time is over I know I am going to a
better place,
but there are no flowers there and no mountain
streams
to cool the day and carry my thoughts away.
Heaven is a beautiful place so I have been told.

When I am gone the sun will still come up
over the Marshes of Glynn golden in its light.
It will travel the length of this great land and
drop from view into the Pacific off Monterey.

People will still stand at Glacier Point and watch
pink alpenglow dance on the crests of the Sierra
Nevada.

The memory of the sight still takes my breath
away.

I shall miss it, but it will not remember me.

The legacy I have will be in my son and those

whom I have loved and served as best I could
here.

That will be beauty enough for me

because there are only plastic flowers where I am
going.

I'll Never Forget Granny

I'll never forget Granny.

Her kindness and gentle spirit are a part of me today.

Her love was unconditional.

I know sometimes I hurt her in the foolishness of my youth,

But she never showed it.

Can I ever follow her example?

I doubt it.

I'm cut from different cloth.

A rough muslin.

She was cut from the finest silk.

Smooth and flowing.

Soft to the touch.

She walked gently through times of tumultuous change.

Born before cars existed.

A simpler time.

No electric lights or indoor plumbing.

"Slop jars" in the night,

And chickens running around under the house
visible through the cracks in the floor.

A thousand stories of the way things used to be.
No, I'll never forget Granny.
She'll always be a part of me.
I'll never be the person she was.
I just hope she's proud of me.

A January Day

High, wispy white clouds in the fading light
await their fate in the oncoming night.
As the cool, cool evening of a January day
surrenders to the darkness that takes them away.

Shadowy forms dance in time with the wind
stretching out their fingers to reach for a friend.
Growing fainter, ever fainter they soon disappear.
When they are gone do you think they were here?

The sky turns pale yellow, then gray fades to
black
like our memories do when someone's love we
lack.
It's like the cool cool evening of a January day
that surrenders to the darkness and takes them
away.

Is Our Love Dying?

How does it feel when love starts to die?
Can you hear it in a voice, or see it in the eyes?
Do you just keep on loving without feeling love?

Tell me if warm, tender lips suddenly grow cold?
Can a lover break your heart and not break your soul?
What are the reasons that I am feeling this pain?

When love starts to die does it happen at night?
Does a home filled with peace end up in a fight?
Is it harder to breathe when you fear it is true?

Are the important things in love the ones that go first?
Not asking or knowing I am not sure which one is worst?
Why does "I Love You" now sound so hollow and trite?

If questions have no answers are they questions at all?
Is our love dashed on the rocks, are we headed for a fall?
What can I say that hasn't already been said?

How does it feel when love starts to die?

Can you hear it in a voice, or see it in the eyes?

If questions have no answers are they questions
at all?

Daddy Bob

My Grandfather wouldn't drive a "City Slicker."
He said it was too big.
The old trolley bus suited him just fine.
He thought that "new bus" was too modern a rig.

He drove the Stone Mountain to Atlanta route
when I was just a kid.
Once and a while he'd let me come along.
It was the neatest thing I ever did.

His bus was small by today's standards.
No it wasn't very big at all.
When I watched Daddy Bob wrestle the steering wheel
I felt I was ten feet tall.

All of his passengers knew my name,
and that made me feel so good.
Daddy Bob bragged about me to everyone
just like I knew he would.

You see I was his little "Beetle Bum."

His very first grandchild.
I've been told that the day I was born
that he nearly went "hog-wild."

He died when I was ten years old.
That was over forty years ago,
and I still miss him every day.
Oh how I loved him so.

When I have passed from this blessed life,
having laid down the tools of this earthly job,
I hope my grandchild thinks of me
like I think of Daddy Bob.

Nate is 16

It seems like another lifetime ago son

when I held you in the palm of my hand.

You were so fragile that I almost wanted to run

and yet the emotions that flooded my heart were grand.

You were my "Beetle Bum."

Your first steps came immediately after that

or so it seemed because time flies when you're amazed.

Soon you were talking. Brilliant words like "dat dat."

The speed of it all even today leaves me dazed.

You were my "Scoot."

The years that followed brought bikes and skateboards

skinned knees and "Watch out for the goosey getter!"

When you were six years old you took Jesus as your Lord.

I knew then that things could only get better and better.

You were my "Cowboy."

Lying down with you until you went to sleep

at the time seemed like such a nuisance.

Made up bedtime stories were all I could do to keep

Awake until you finally let rest compound your innocence.

You were my "Snuggle Buddy."

School and T-ball games and the next time I looked

you were starting to talk about those girls you used to hate.

It seems that the thing that was once most detestable had you hooked

And then you wanted to start to go out on dates.

You were my "Killer."

I could go on and on these years because they have really been unique.

Each one holds a special moment and memory.

As I sit here writing these lines I've let my heart speak

those things I have pondered there so secretly.

You are my son but most of all my friend.

Papa's Chair

I still have Papa's chair.
It's been re-covered, but it's still his.
When I sit in it I can feel his presence.
The memories of him pour in like a flood.
I let them carry me away.

Papa loved "Live Atlanta Wrestling."
He thought it was real.
Dick the Bruiser and the Assassins
were his companions every Saturday night.
Remember two falls, or a TV time limit?

I carry the wisdom he dispensed from that chair today.
"Get your books," he'd say,
and I knew to study hard.
"Boy, you'd tear up the Iron Devil."
Be careful. Things do break.

Papa was quick with a joke.
He knew a million of them.
Those he called "smutty tales"

were mild by today's standards.
I'd love to hear him tell one now.

Yes I still have Papa's chair:
And if that was all I had I'd be sad.
But I have much, much more.
I have his memories,
and I'll never re-cover those.

For Judy

Once I was alone.
I had no friends to laugh with me, to cry with me,
or to share my dreams…
Then I met you
and my life turned from a joke
into something real.

The wonderment of it all numbs my mind
and thrills me to the bone.
What was once ugly and empty
is now beautiful and full of life.

The broad awakening that someone
could really change my life.
I'm happy.

Nanny Pat

I was blessed to have a grandmother like Nanny
Pat.

Every time I think of her I think of hats.

Lady-like hats that showed her style and grace

and oh yes, every hair was always in its place.

Many fond memories of times long past

mix with new ones like Saint Patty's day last

when we took her to our favorite place to eat.

The baked Alaska and joy we shared was really
sweet.

When things were tough for me she was always
there.

With a kind and comforting word she showed
she cared.

Without her love I don't think I'd have made it
through.

Hers was a grandmother's love that was real and
oh so very true.

Words on a page will never be able to express

The things I feel for her and my gratefulness

That she was always in my corner through thick and thin.

Although she was my grandmother she is my truest friend.

(Author's Note: Nanny Pat died a few years ago. I still miss her today. She was an amazing, Southern lady in every way. I'm so glad the separation is only temporary.)

Give Love a Whirl

Love is as love does
or so the saying goes.
What makes a person fall in love?
Nobody really knows.

With some it starts with an innocent glance.
With others a wink and a smile
And before you know it you're head over heels.
Yes you're finished: truly beguiled.

Many have thought about love.
Some have even tried to define
its peculiar twists and turns.
Many have lost their love and their minds.

But to those who find it love is a rose
that's more beautiful than the purest pearl.
Part of the joy is the search and the chase
so come on, take the plunge, give love a whirl.

The Irony of It

I see things in black and white.
You see them in shades of gray
As somewhat defined objects dancing in the mist.
Both of us are right and that's the irony of it.

Talk is cheap when it's not from the heart.
Communication fades to black,
and with it any hope of understanding.
Both of us are wrong and that's the irony of it.

Sometimes this dilemma causes us pain.
The anger ebbs and flows like the Gulf
as it laps against our emotions.
Both of us are hurt and that's the irony of it.

The longer we're together the closer we get.
The paradox of it all is astounding.
The very things that separate also bind.
Both of us are in love and that's the irony of it.

The Unanswered Door

I stand outside your door
all misty wet with rain.
The silent fog rolls across the glen
and you won't let me in.

In its grayness I stand alone
lost in musings of you.
Darkness descends on my heart.
As you know it does when we are apart.

The walk is pink with petals
of a spring that has taken leave.
I soon will need to do likewise.
O to look once more into your eyes.

In your eyes I have seen
the reflection of the heather's bloom.
In the valley by the ancient stream
when things were what they seemed.

We were younger then.
Hope filled, and by dreams inspired.

We walked through the vale hand in hand
and sat on it's bank in the cool, moist sand.

I long to close my eyes.
Please take me to those days
when living was as simple.
And love was easy and free.

The mist is turning to rain
as the faint shadows fade.
Turning up my collar against the chill
I am gone and yet I love you still.

By the Sea in Winter

I walked beside the sea in winter.

The wind blew and the waves crashed among the rock.

The spray hit my face.

It felt like needles and I turned away.

It was a lonely, wondrous place.

The gulls cried their lonely cries.

They circled as best they could in the winter gale.

They dived for their food,

and rose again with their prize.

Their cries seemed to set my mood.

The roar of the surf was comforting.

The sound rose and fell like a woman's breasts as she sleeps.

Back and forth, in and out

went the sea on its endless journey.

It was beautiful. No doubt.

I was lost in my thoughts of you.

They rose and fell and crashed into my mind.

Warming me like the sun above.

You are like the sea.

Beautiful, and I am in love.

The Campfire

I built a campfire the other evening.

We were camping and the night air was cool.

It had been a long time and I had almost forgotten.

How could I have been such a fool?

The glow of the fire illumined our faces

As the sparks floated off to compete with the stars.

The kids moved away and we were left alone

Your head on my shoulder began to heal the scars.

I'd been foolish and hurt, in many ways a child.

Harbored bitterness and I'm ashamed to say hate.

Knowing better doesn't always mean we do.

Once the healing starts you realize there is a better fate.

We snuggled under the blanket.

Closer than we had been in a long, long time.

Not physically but spiritually we linked up again,

The road ahead may not be smooth, but it will be fine.

Life is a puzzle that has many missing parts.

We struggle to find them all and sometimes lose our hearts.

The picture is still just as beautiful if we can only see

That it's the joy of working the puzzle together that really sets us free.

Thoughts of You at Laguna Beach

The rainbow formed on the edge of the rain

And its colors seemed to glow;

Like a million fireflies they danced, row upon row.

The red-pink hues of fading sunlight cut across its stain.

A hummingbird appeared out of nowhere.

I didn't see it fly up over the cliff.

It hovered in the air resisting the urge to drift.

A few moments ago it seemed to materialize there.

The deep green ocean crowns the visual feast.

Waves run at slight angles to the horizon

Racing away as if they are afraid of the setting sun.

Right now I am sure that of all creatures I am the least.

I am transfixed by this moment in time

Knowing that soon it will end.

I am sad because you are not here my love, my
friend,

And in the mysterious things of the heart that is a
crime.

A Paradoxical Son of the South

I am a paradoxical son of the South.

Proud of my heritage. Saddened by what I see.

I am appalled by racism and all things associated with it

Yet I sometimes cry when I see the "Stars and Bars."

It's not a racist symbol to me.

I am thankful that all men are free.

I have a strong dislike (I despise the word hate),

For those who have taken something noble

And prostituted it for their evil ends.

They are weak and cowardly men

Who have to hide behind a sheet or baldhead and leather

To spew their lies and fear in the summer heat.

My ancestors bled and died for that cause so long ago.

They were simple men. Farmers. They never owned a slave.

Like most who wore the gray they weren't idealists.

They loved the South, as I do, and were willing to

Pay the highest price for that love. Would I?

That price seems in retrospect too high.

Yes, I am a paradoxical son of the South.

A true son. Proud and strong; yet different from the cowards.

Willing to walk with my brothers of color.

To eat with them and entertain them as guests in my home.

The cowards don't understand. I doubt they ever will.

For them the truth is a bitter, bitter pill.

Time. The Sun.

Light bright lines in the fading sunset
Strike my eyes until I am blinded by its beauty.
Quiet reds and yellows of the evening sun
Remind me of the fleeting ship of time.

Time moves at a snail's pace
Like the shadows of the setting sun.
Time, like the sun, will soon be gone
Leaving us only memories.
Memories of the sun.

The Literary Dilemma

I tried to write a poem today.

That's tough when you don't have much to say.

I've thought about it all day.

Ever since I rose from the hay,

But I can't seem to get it underway.

It's good that I don't do this for pay.

So I'll just keep trying come what may.

Keep searching for the rhyme that got away.

Thoughts Aroused By A Glance

I catch you out of the corner of my eye
And I take a quick, cautious glance at you.
Your brown skin causes me to tense up
With fear at first, and then anger, at myself.

Why do I react this way when I see you?
What is it within me that causes this reaction?
It makes me angry and sad that sometimes these
Feelings still exist no matter how hard I try.

Do you feel the same way when you see me lily-
white?
God knows you have more of a right than I
To have this primeval fear steal the very breath
From your throat and cause your heart to pound.

Deep in your minds darkest recesses the
memories
Of another place and another time must still
reside.
Bullwhips crack and women and children cry
because

Their men have been torn away and sold, or worse.

I don't blame you for the way you must feel,

And I'm sorry for the pain it probably still causes you.

Help me to understand my feelings of fear,

Or is it guilt for something I never did.

Do you know?

Somewhere the cycle of separation must be broken.

Somehow we both have to exorcise our demons

Before they consume us, or consume us they will.

The demons of hatred and racism love us neither one.

We must then learn to love each other to survive.

Servant of the Machine

I am a servant of the machine.

Unthinking, unseeing I move about.

Trapped in a world I love-hate I live.

A blind-dumb blob I live.

Or do I?

The Unknown

I walked on hallowed ground today.

It had been quite a while since I'd passed that way.

The tombstones stood at attention; tall and white

As the failing day struggled with the oncoming night.

I stood with my hands on the unknown's tomb,

And wondered who lay in its cold, dark womb

Awaiting that great and glorious day

When the dead will rise to be on their way.

Did his mother weep a mournful tear

When she was finally captured by her worst fear?

Did she lie awake at night in her bed

And tremble at the thought that her boy was dead?

Did he have a wife and a family?

Was his dying thought to with her be?

Did he long to lay his head on her breast

As the specter of death stole away his breath?

I stood there a long time lost in my thoughts

Of this unknown soul and his cause that is lost.

It was as dark as my mood as I walked away.

A good man was long since gone; there was
nothing to say.

A Noble Quest

Wisdom is a quality not found in great abundance.

It appears in the most unusual places.

In the drunk who lies down to sleep over the sewer grate,

Or the child who loves all with no regard to race.

Truth is the mystery of all mysteries.

Its pretenders are everywhere crying out to all.

From the politician who will promise you anything for a vote

To the charlatan whose words still ring out as he falls.

Love. True unconditional love is even more scarce.

Very few are willing to bare their chests in its name.

The simple carpenter who touched the world in His darkest moment did.

Indeed He did but to most even that is just a game.

There is hope in this world. I believe it to be
true.

Seek wisdom everywhere it can be found.

Live truth in even the smallest aspects of life,

And cherish love for in its thorns true
contentment abounds.

The Actor

I am an actor on the great stage.

The superstar of one of the greatest tragedies of all time…

My life.

I always give a superb performance.

Playing each scene to the greatest of my ability…

I cry.

I work the audience.

Building them up to a crescendo of emotion

Which leads to thundering applause

At the final curtain…

My death.

Night Sky

When I stare into the white speckled indigo of the night sky I realize that I am nothing.

A mere microbe in the universe; Invisible to all except You and Your all-seeing eye.

Yet You, in Your immeasurable compassion, reached across the vastness of space to touch the human race.

A meteorite spins through the cold thin air leaving a trail of fire and then it is gone.

It reminds me of You and Your short visit here. Your fire left behind, unlike the meteorite's, doesn't fade.

The reality of You and the fire that still burns brightly in those who belong to You is comforting.

The moon is a yellow-orange balloon setting the tops of the trees ablaze on the horizon.

It slowly creeps up into the night sky as if trying to be unnoticed by those of us watching.

Its brightness soon becomes a beacon to all who see it like Your words are to those who choose to hear them.

Let me be found among those who hear Your words and follow after them as after life itself.

For as I stare into the white speckled indigo of the night sky I realize that without You I am nothing.

The Remnants of the Day

I savor the remnants of the day.

Late in the evening when the sun is low,

And shadows are long.

Recollections of the past come my way.

They drift by ever so slowly,

And though not all good they are never wrong.

I'm warmed by memories passing.

Strangely warmed by the fires they kindle.

Like a beggar who finds a blanket on a cold night

I cling to the joy they bring.

As the light from the setting sun begins to
dwindle.

Soon it's gone, as they are, but all is right.

I savor the remnants of the day.

Everyday.

The Lament of the Ancient Poet

The ancient poet screamed out his warning,

But it went unheeded in the roar of the masses.

His wrinkled face was scarred with the sadness of a thousand years of loneliness.

The loneliness of truth.

On he walked in a sea of blank faces.

"Listen!" He cried, but no one heard.

Suddenly he grasped his chest.

He stumbled and fell into the ever-moving motion of humanity.

The poet died.

The poet died, and with him truth.

Truth trampled into silence by the flow of lies.

Humanity's lies.

Rebel Soldiers

Death, like a dark veil, surrounds the men of old.

It covers the brave man and the coward.

It hides the timid man and the bold.

Time has passed them in their tombs.

The glory is gone, vanished in the shadows of
doom.

The things they've said and things they've done

have disappeared like a bird that flies toward the
sun.

Their battle flags and combat's lust?

There's nothing left but dust.

Terry R. Freeman

The Road

The tops of the trees glow like coals
As I drive East into the coming night.
Thoughts of you fill my head like
The beauty of a winter day's fading light.

Where are you now I said out loud
As the sun slowly falls at my back.
No one answered because no one was
There and the blue sky gives way to black.

I've struggled through my life since I left
you like a blind man lost in a maze.
Groping along, just running on feelings
As the long hours turned into longer days.

You're as gone as the sun, as I drive
Alone into the ever deepening night.
The road is a ribbon of lines and signs
That will lead me on East toward the coming
light.

Blind Fingers

Blind fingers groping blindly through the stench-filled night.

Thrown to the depths of despair by their blindness they wander.

Aimlessly.

Searching but never finding anything but another piece of trash.

Would they be better if they could see?

Would that make them clean?

No.

They are better left to stumble through the filth unseeing.

It is you and I who are trapped my friend.

We slosh through the refuse daily.

Always seeing, always feeling, but never cleaning up what we ourselves have done.

We have become numb to the scum just like blind fingers.

Fall

Beautiful mountain scenes splashed in colors of every imaginable hue.

A living-dying canvas painted by the Master Painter.

A silent, breathtaking, testimony for the living God.

A masterpiece of His creation.

Fall.

Forgiven

I drove the nails into His hands.

I pressed the thorns into His brow.

I dropped the cross into the hole.

I spat on Him.

I gambled for His clothes

I took a spear and pierced His precious side.

Yet He loves me.

I am Forgiven.

Praise!

I lived my life all out of time.

Without reason and without rhyme

Until I made the Savior mine.

Now my life really shines.

Thank you Jesus.

No more confusion.

No more sin.

Since I asked my Jesus in.

Old things are gone.

Now all things are new.

Praise you Jesus.

I love you!

Thank you Lord!

Not Alone

A storm was moving in fast from the West.

The sky quickly turned as yellow as a daffodil.

An eerie silence pulled itself over the land like a
blanket,

And I was alone.

The wind began to blow with a cool breath.

Leaves swirled and danced at its command.

Rain began to fall slowly at first and then in
buckets,

And I was alone

Limbs broke loose and crashed to the ground.

Their twigs blew free and scratched my bare face.

The sky turned as black and foreboding as death,

And I was alone.

It started to hail and soon the ground was white.

The wind blew stronger still and began to moan.

Thunder rolled and lightening flashed in my eyes,

And I was alone.

Just as suddenly the sky grew brighter.

The cold rain slowed to a drizzle.

A rainbow appeared out of nowhere in the Eastern sky…

I am not alone.

Submission

Sweet Holy Spirit touch my life.

Come in and take control.

Fill me with Your precious love.

Come in and thrill my very soul.

I need Your power in my life

To take away all sin and strife.

Descend on me precious dove,

And fill me with Your warm sweet love.

(Author's Note: This simple little poem of praise became a song, "My Submission", in the skillful hands of my precious friend Russell Davis. Our Gospel group sang it for years afterward. Russell pastors a church near Monroe, Georgia. He is still my dearest friend and a source of constant strength and inspiration to me.)

Habitations of Dragons

I have seen the habitations of dragons.

The dark and bone-filled places where they live.

I have been to the deepest caverns

Where the know-light has never penetrated.

Laid down and went to sleep, I have,

Not fearing the darkness or the sulfurous heavy breathing.

Dragons don't mean anything to me

For I know the Dragonslayer.

He is my friend.

I am his bond-servant.

The dragon's fire may scorch my flesh but I'll not burn.

The sweet potions He supplies heal the pain.

I've never seen the Dragonslayer,

But I know He is here

In me and that is enough

For now.

It won't be long until I see Him,

And when I do the dragons will all be gone.

Forever.

Yosemite at Eventide

I stood on Glacier Point at sunset.

The shadows crawled slowly up the mountains.

They rolled over the tops of the peaks,

And spilled onto the valley floor.

Yosemite at eventide.

Your presence is everywhere.

Time slows down as nature speaks.

The alpenglow with pinkish hue

Is painted across the Sierra Nevada.

The setting sun has done this.

In the quiet of the moment

I hear the twin falls, Nevada and Vernal.

Their water that once was snow

Crashes to the rocks with a hiss.

I am alone with my thoughts

Though people are all around me.

It's very hard to breathe.

Is it the altitude or the impact of

Your canvas that is ever changing before my
eyes?

Yosemite at eventide.

I don't ever want to leave.

The Dream

Dancing on the crest of a dream; or is it real?

I see the sun spinning across the horizon wearing a smile.

Surreal is reality; At least that is how I feel.

I wonder if I'd like to stay here for a while.

The forest breathes its breath of love upon me.

I am overcome by the powerful, pungent aroma.

Slipping, I fall backwards into a swirling emotional sea

Grasping wildly at reality's straws as I slip into a coma.

Just now I heard the sound of your breathing.

Or was that the roar of a toilet being flushed?

This is strange; I can't believe what I'm seeing.

Lenny Bruce shaking hands with Ben Franklin's bust.

The brilliant colors run together like a fire at a wax museum.

Someone pulled the plug and they dribble down the drain.

Suddenly cold air blasts my neck as they open the mausoleum.

Terry R. Freeman

I turn around in the sticky wax to see the face of pain.

I try to run but my feet are stuck to the beautiful floor.

Breaking free I race up the dark creaky stairs.

When I reach the hallway there are several doors.

Choosing one I rush in and fall headlong into thin air.

I awake with a start and sit bolt upright in bed.

Breathing is hard as my eyes adjust to the light.

The fact that it's my room sinks slowly into my head.

Lying back on the wet pillow I prepare to reenter the night.

84

The Fool

He stood alone on the street that night
As a cold rain was gently falling down.
Trembling in the shadows of a lonely street light
In a dangerous part of town.

It was almost midnight and the subculture
Was beginning to awaken and move about.
The letters on the cardboard sign he held were
running.
He was crazy I had no doubt.

Well I've always been the curious type
And this man was strangely intriguing.
So I pulled up my collar and started his way
When to my surprise he started singing.

It was a song I knew from long ago.
Yes I remembered it from Sunday School.
"Jesus loves me this I know," he sang.
I just stopped and stared at the fool.

The street people parted when they got close
But he just looked at them and smiled.
He had the funniest look on his face.
It reminded me of a little child.

I walked on over and stood close by
Just to listen for a while.
Some people made threats and cursed at him but
he ignored them.
He seemed so meek and mild.

I stood and watched for as long as I could
Then stepped from my dark place into his light.
I said, "Man do you really think you're going
To change the world on this street, right here,
tonight?"

I startled him with my question I guess.
He whirled around so that's what it had to be.
He said, "I suppose not, but I just want to make
Sure that the world doesn't change me."

The Magic Sword

We all have our dragons to fight.

At times they seem to fall from the sky.

Large, and circling down on leathery wings

Breathing fire and bellowing smoke.

Those are the easy ones.

You can see them coming.

It's the ones who suddenly appear

Without warning that hurt the most.

Poof, and there they are

And before you know it you're burned.

I hate those.

Yes, we all have our dragons to fight.

Thank God for the magic sword.

A Walk In A Summer Rain

I saw Your face in the midst of the clouds today.

They were black and swirling

When a shaft of bright white light broke through

And there You were.

You are the light in a dark place.

I felt Your gentle touch while standing in the rain today.

A warm summer shower was falling.

I walked out into it

And Your arms enfolded me.

You are water in a dry and weary land.

I saw something that reminded me of Your love in a stream today.

It was swollen from the rain,

And the flotsam danced away in the rushing water

Leaving the bank shiny and clean.

Your love pours over me and washes me clean.

Getting Back to "We"

It is "we" that I long for.
"I" is just too much to bare.
With "I" self doubt reigns.
"We" causes joy to fill the air.

Once "we" was all there was
And all there needed to be.
How did "I" rear its ill-favored head?
Was I just too blind to see?

"I am nothing without You," I want to say.
Why is that so hard to face?
Lord breathe Your breath of love,
And let it cover me with Your grace.

"I" reluctantly bows before You now
Gradually giving way to "we".
Come pour Your wine upon my heart.
Touch my eyes that I might see.

Heavenly Baby, Holy Child

Heavenly Baby, Holy Child
Born so lowly, meek and mild.
Tender Child, heaven's best
Come to die for all the rest.

God's provision for my soul,
Births' foretold since days of old.
Lay so still in the crystal night
Has come to lead us to the light.

Baby Jesus at Mary's breast
Wise men and shepherds blessed.
The animals all stood round in awe
Calmed by everything they saw.

In that manger so long ago
My Savior came so I could know
His Father as He did; my own
And worship Him around His throne.

Heavenly baby, Holy Child
Born so lowly, meek and mild.

Tender Child, heaven's best

Come to die for all the rest.

Terry R. Freeman

The Chains Are Falling

The chains are falling
From my ankles and wrists.
A sense of peace replaces fists.
Blinded eyes now are opened to the light.
What has been wrong is now becoming right.
The chains are falling.

The chains are falling;
They crumble at my feet.
Praise replaces words I won't repeat.
A spirit broken now soars upward to the Son.
Living water flows; the work is being done.
The chains are falling.

The chains are falling
Finally powerless at my side.
Freedom awaits me at the end of this ride.
A bitter struggle is ending inside of me
The years of bondage are over; I am free.
The chains are falling.

Musings

Life is like the curve of a waterfall.
Ever changing but always the same.
Sometimes big and sometimes small,
Sometimes wild and sometimes tame.

Flow is most important as we go along.
Motion without movement is the key.
Impact on the rocks make the song.
Struggling to get loose we are free.

Early Spring Morning

Green fields of grass veiled by mist
shimmering in the day's first light.
Songbirds singing their morning song
as the day overpowers the night.

Thoughts of you appear in my coffee's steam
floating there in the soft morning.
I am captured by the look on your face
in the golden mists of the dawning.

Come away with me to that distant shore
your eyes seem to say without words.
We'll lie together on the warm white sand,
and tell stories that we've never heard.

Small talk that seemed meaningless at the time
now looms large; I hang on your every word.
The sea's song mingles with your words until
they become one.
It's the song of the ages, or so I've heard.

The coffee is gone and the sun is warm.

The sweat runs down the small of my back.

I gather my things and retreat to the house,

fortified by the memory that keeps me on track.

Terry R. Freeman

His Hold is Light

Success is found in His grip.
His hold is light.
And there is great joy in the trip.

Life is not a destination you see.
There are twists and turns.
You never really "get there" until you're free.

Striving and stressing just makes you old.
It's not the gray hair.
In fact, the gray hair should be a goal.

Each graying strand is filled with wisdom
born of experience.
Love, hate, joy and sadness make the sum.

Time passes quickly; "poof" it's gone.
"Somebody stop the bus!"
Don't strain to hear the melody and miss the
song.

Remember, success is found in His grip.

His hold is light.

And there is great joy in the trip

Wolffork Valley

Its cool as the sun peeks over Rabun Ridge.
Below is fog all cottony white.
The steeple of the church just visible
In the early morning's light.

Cows call to each other,
And up near Blue Ridge Gap Road a rooster crows.
An ancient ritual, peaceful and primeval;
But how do they know?

The mountains are all on fire.
Colors. Orange, Red, and Yellow in every hue.
Smokehouse Knob, Black Rock, Walnut,
Rabun Bald, and Charlie Mountain too.

The farms and fields come into view
As the fog gives way to the sun.
Like an antique patchwork quilt they
Seem they are not real, but spun.

The hand of God is at work
As Fall overtakes Wolffork Valley.
His masterful handiwork is clear,
And the evidence too much to tally.